ELITE FORCES SURVIVAL GUIDE SERIES

Elite Survival
Survive in the Desert with the French Foreign Legion
Survive in the Arctic with the Royal Marine Commandos
Survive in the Mountains with the U.S. Rangers and Army
 Mountain Division
Survive in the Jungle with the Special Forces "Green Berets"
Survive in the Wilderness with the Canadian and Australian
 Special Forces
Survive at Sea with the U.S. Navy SEALs
Training to Fight with the Parachute Regiment
The World's Best Soldiers

Elite Operations and Training
Escape and Evasion
Surviving Captivity with the U.S. Air Force
Hostage Rescue with the SAS
How to Pass Elite Forces Selection
Learning Mental Endurance with the U.S. Marines

Special Forces Survival Guidebooks
Survival Equipment
Navigation and Signaling
Surviving Natural Disasters
Using Ropes and Knots
Survival First Aid
Trapping, Fishing, and Plant Food
Urban Survival Techniques

SURVIVE IN THE ARCTIC WITH THE ROYAL MARINE COMMANDOS

CHRIS McNAB

Introduction by Colonel John T. Carney. Jr., USAF–Ret.
President, Special Operations Warrior Foundation

MASON CREST PUBLISHERS

This edition first published in 2003
by Mason Crest Publishers Inc.
370 Reed Road, Broomall, PA, 19008

Library of Congress Cataloging-in-Publication Data available

ISBN 1-59084-002-X

Editorial and design by
Amber Books Ltd.
Bradley's Close
74–77 White Lion Street
London N1 9PF

Project Editor Chris Stone
Designer Simon Thompson
Picture Research Lisa Wren

Printed and bound in Malaysia

10 9 8 7 6 5 4 3 2 1

ACKNOWLEDGMENT
For authenticating this book, the Publishers would like to thank the Public Affairs Offices of the U.S. Special Operations Command, MacDill AFB, FL.; Army Special Operations Command, Fort Bragg, N.C.; Navy Special Warfare Command, Coronado, CA.; and the Air Force Special Operations Command, Hurlbert Field, FL.

T   104638

IMPORTANT NOTICE
The survival techniques and information described in this publication are for use in dire circumstances where the safety of the individual is at risk. Accordingly, the publisher cannot accept any responsibility for any prosecution or proceedings brought or instituted against any person or body as a result of the uses or misuses of the techniques and information within.

DEDICATION
This book is dedicated to those who perished in the terrorist attacks of September 11, 2001, and to the Special Forces soldiers who continually serve to defend freedom.

Picture Credits
Corbis: 20, 23, 30, 48, 50, 68, 82; **Military Picture Library**: 18, 24, 34, 38, 42, 46, 54, 58, 62, 71, 72, 78, 81, 89; **TRH**: 6, , 8, 11, 14, 15, 16, 26, 36, 57, 60, 61, 63, 69, 73, 75, 84, 88
llustrations courtesy of Amber Books and De Agostini UK
Front cover: **MPL** (inset), **Corbis** (main)

CONTENTS

Introduction   6

The Arctic Warriors   8

The Polar Regions   18

Shelter   24

Making Fire   36

Finding Food   46

Traveling and Navigation   58

Clothing   66

Dangers and First Aid   78

Glossary   90

Equipment Requirements   92

Chronology   93

Recruitment Information   94

Further Reading/About the Author   95

Index   96

INTRODUCTION

Elite forces are the tip of Freedom's spear. These small, special units are universally the first to engage, whether on reconnaissance missions into denied territory for larger, conventional forces or in direct action, surgical operations, preemptive strikes, retaliatory action, and hostage rescues. They lead the way in today's war on terrorism, the war on drugs, the war on transnational unrest, and in humanitarian operations as well as nation building. When large scale warfare erupts, they offer theater commanders a wide variety of unique, unconventional options.

Most such units are regionally oriented, acclimated to the culture and conversant in the languages of the areas where they operate. Since they deploy to those areas regularly, often for combined training exercises with indigenous forces, these elite units also serve as peacetime "global scouts" and "diplomacy multipliers," a beacon of hope for the democratic aspirations of oppressed peoples all over the globe.

Elite forces are truly "quiet professionals": their actions speak louder than words. They are self-motivated, self-confident, versatile, seasoned, mature individuals who rely on teamwork more than daring-do. Unfortunately, theirs is dangerous work. Since "Desert One"—the 1980 attempt to rescue hostages from the U.S. embassy in Tehran, for instance—American special operations forces have suffered casualties in real world operations at close to fifteen times the rate of U.S. conventional forces. By the very nature of the challenges which face special operations forces, training for these elite units has proven even more hazardous.

Thus it's with special pride that I join you in saluting the brave men and women who volunteer to serve in and support these magnificent units and who face such difficult challenges ahead.

Colonel John T. Carney, Jr., USAF–Ret.
President, Special Operations Warrior Foundation

Soldiers of the Mountain and Arctic Warfare Cadre, a specialized squad within the No.3 Commando Brigade of the Royal Marines.

THE ARCTIC WARRIORS

The Royal Marine Commandos are one of the world's oldest elite units. Since 1664 they have shown incredible bravery in battles from the jungles of the Far East to the icy South Atlantic.

The Royal Marine Commandos have a history of courage under fire. They have fought with honor in deserts, jungles, forests, and on beaches. Yet they are perhaps most famous as arctic warriors. Every Royal Marine is trained in the arctic snows of Norway, so we can learn from them how to survive in subzero temperatures. But first, let us look at their history in battle.

The first British Marine unit of 1,200 soldiers was formed on October 28, 1664, in London, England. They were first known as the Duke of York and Albany's Maritime Regiment of Foot. Then they quickly became known as the Lord High Admiral's Regiment. These "sea soldiers" were sent into the Royal Navy to provide snipers, and to repel enemy boarding parties during the fierce naval engagements of the Second and Third Dutch Wars. They were also deployed as landing parties, and to maintain discipline aboard the ships. In 1802 King George III formally renamed them the Royal Marines.

The Marines fought hard in both world wars. In World War I, Marines served in the muddy trenches of the Western Front, and also attacked a German U-boat base in Belgium in a daring

Royal Marines using skis to get around. There are only 6,000 Royal Marines in active service; their training period lasts 42 weeks.

amphibious raid. In World War II, an elite unit within the Royal Marines—the Royal Marine Commandos—was formed to serve alongside commando units from the British Army. The Royal Marine Commandos saw their first action on the bloody beaches of **Dieppe** in German-occupied France in August 1942. The attack was a rehearsal for the **D-Day** landings. The commandos attacked huge German coastal guns with great bravery and violence. Although there were heavy casualties among the infantry on the raid, the commando operations enjoyed reasonable success. Because of this, RM Commandos were later used when the Allies invaded France in June 1944.

The job of the Commandos on D-Day was to help destroy a section of the German **Atlantic Wall**. This was a series of German coastal fortifications surrounded by minefields, and defended by artillery and infantry. On June 6, 1944, the Commandos landed on the beaches of France. The fight was hard. The Marines had to battle their

A Royal Marine on patrol in World War II carries a 9-mm Thompson submachine gun, with ammunition packs on his belt.

way off of the beaches through hails of machine-gun fire that split the air. Then they had to fight house by house, field by field, and garden by garden for days at a time under a relentless German counter-attack, sometimes fighting hand-to-hand with German soldiers. Some of the Commandos battled without sleep for more than three days, and gained the Germans' respect by doing so. Despite some commando units losing up to half of their men, they

This boat is a special Landing Craft Assault (LCA) vehicle which could carry 35 fully armed Royal Marines onto enemy beaches.

never surrendered. The RM Commandos fought across France, Holland, Belgium, and into Germany, and they became legendary as tough men who faced death and danger without flinching.

In the years following World War II the Royal Marines were still involved in many military operations. In 1956, RM Commandos took part in a British and French operation in Egypt to capture an important waterway called the Suez Canal. During this operation some Commandos went into battle against the city of Port Said by boats. (This is known as an "amphibious assault.") Others attacked Port Said using fast landings by helicopter. Over several days, Egyptian troops were cleared from the city by the Commandos and British Paras, supported by the Centurion tanks of the Royal Tank Regiment, aircraft of the Fleet Air Arm, and naval gunfire. The Royal Marines were heavily involved in the unpleasant business of house-clearing, which cost them a total of nine dead and 60 wounded.

After the battle in Egypt, the RM Commandos found themselves fighting in many more hot climates, including the jungles of Malaysia and Indonesia. Yet in April 1982, they were sent to a place with a climate at the opposite extreme. A major conflict developed in the South Atlantic when Argentinian forces invaded the British Falkland Islands, and claimed them as Argentine territory. The Royal Marines were duly summoned to head the task force that intended to recapture the islands.

The Falkland Islands are a cold and forbidding place, not far from the icy wastes of **Antarctica**. Once the Marines had landed on the islands, their job was to advance across the island,

and help recapture the islands' capital, Port Stanley. Ahead lay a series of Argentine mountaintop positions held by up to 9,000 soldiers in often superb defensive positions. The Marines also had to try to stay alive under subzero temperatures, and bitterly cold rain and **blizzards**.

The battles to take the mountains of the Falklands were hard and brutal. The Marines faced heavy machine-gun fire and constant explosions, and they had to fight for every inch of ground. They were usually outnumbered by Argentinian forces, but through cunning and courage they overcame each position they encountered. Finally they were able to enter Port Stanley, leaving many dead behind them but making sure that their legendary status was enhanced.

A Royal Marine during the Falklands War in 1982 carries an L4A4 weapon, one of the world's most accurate machine guns.

The experience of fighting in the cold climate of the Falklands taught the Royal Marines many valuable lessons about survival in polar regions. They put these lessons to use by creating new units dedicated to arctic combat and survival. Based in Scotland, 45 Commando was the first unit to specialize in cold-weather warfare, carrying out regular training in Norway, a place renowned for its harsh arctic climate. In the 1970s they were joined by 42 Commando, forming the core of a British ski-borne force trained in mountain and arctic warfare. These soldiers were trained to hold out against any possible Soviet attacks through the icy regions of northern Europe during the conflict known as the "**Cold War.**"

Apart from machine guns, each Commando unit in the Falklands War was equipped with 24 MILAN antitank rockets and 18 mortars.

Special Boat Service (SBS) soldiers are all volunteers from the RM Commandos and they do a 15-week course in amphibious combat.

The Royal Marines also have a number of smaller units for special missions in arctic environments. The **Mountain and Arctic Warfare Cadre** (M&AWC) was formed to teach the Commandos arctic warfare, and provide instruction in cliff and mountain climbing. Trained to survive the unfriendly environment of the Norwegian wilderness in winter, the Cadre excelled in the Falkland Islands. The other highly specialized unit deployed by the Royal Marines is their Special Boat Squadron (SBS), now renamed the **Special Boat Service**. This is one of the world's most secret units.

Many people would say that they are as good as the SAS (Britain's Special Air Service), and some would say they are even better. Today's SBS operator is a highly trained swimmer/canoeist and parachutist capable of performing a variety of missions, even in

Royal Marines stand by a BV202 armored vehicle. If the vehicle is full with equipment, the Marines will be towed behind on their skis.

MARK OF THE COMMANDO

All commando-trained soldiers wear the famous green beret—it marks them out from other units. The army and support units wear their own cap badge with their own regimental emblems, while the Royal Marines beret badge is the "Great Globe" encircled with laurel, and bearing the Latin motto *Per Mare, Per Terram*. This means "By Sea, By Land"—and it shows that the Marines can fight anywhere. Their history proves that they can do just that.

arctic waters. In the Falklands they swam or sailed through the freezing waters of the South Atlantic to take up hiding positions only feet from the Argentinian army positions. They even managed to infiltrate the old shipwreck of the *Lady Elizabeth* in Stanley Harbour. From their cold, damp vantage point, the patrol reported back on the Argentinian movements to the other British forces.

All Royal Marine recruits must do part of their training in Norway. Consequently, their experience of surviving in arctic conditions is vast, and they are some of the world's best instructors in arctic survival. They must know how to survive if they are stranded in the middle of a snowy landscape in temperatures well below freezing. They must know what to do if they fall through ice into subzero waters. And they must understand how to acquire food when all there seems to be is snow and ice. How they do all this is the lesson of this book.

THE POLAR REGIONS

The two polar ice caps are the coldest places on Earth, and survival there is difficult. Yet polar conditions can exist even outside of these regions.

When we speak of arctic survival, we are strictly speaking about the polar ice caps in the far north and far south of the planet. The north polar region is a frozen ocean, the Arctic Ocean. The south polar region, or Antarctic continent, is a land mass which is extremely cold, and almost entirely covered by ice. This ice can be up to an amazing 10,000 feet (3 km) thick!

In the polar regions during the winter, the sun can remain below the horizon for several months, so that the only source of warmth is wind flowing in from warmer latitudes. In the summer, the sun remains low in the sky and provides little heat, although over the **Arctic** Circle the sun is above the horizon 24 hours a day for part of the summer. This means no nighttime! The Antarctic continent supports only two species of flowering plant, and the animals in the polar regions are almost entirely dependent on the sea for food. There are almost no land animals in the Antarctic, but the polar bear lives in the Arctic. Birds come to some areas of the Arctic in the summer to breed. Seals can be found in both regions, and penguins are a typical animal of Antarctica.

Marines are dropped off on exercises by a Westland Sea King helicopter which can carry a full-armed patrol for 764 miles (1,230 km).

Yet arctic-type weather is found not only in these two regions. The Royal Marines are also trained to survive anywhere where the temperature is below freezing, such as mountains or winter woodlands. There are two types of cold-weather areas: snow climates and ice climates. Snow climates are found between the Arctic and Antarctic. Snow areas are usually covered by needle-leaf forests, with an abundance of lakes and swamps. The coastlines vary from gentle plains sweeping down to the sea, to steep, rugged cliffs with glaciers at high altitudes. Vegetation ranges from cedar, spruce, fir, and pine trees to dwarf willow, birch, and alder nearer the **tundra** line. Snow climates are characterized by vast extremes, with temperatures ranging from –45°F (–43°C) in the winter to 110°F (44°C) in the summer. In some places, such as parts of

It is easy to be lost in the Arctic. The Arctic ice sheet surrounding the north pole is 670,000 square miles (1,740,000 sq km) in size.

PROBLEMS OF TRAVELING IN POLAR REGIONS

- Poor visibility makes navigation difficult. A compass is essential, but the different magnetic conditions at the poles can make them less accurate.
- In summer, there will be a mass of bogs, swamps, and standing water, which are difficult to cross. They are accompanied by lots of mosquitoes, which will bite you if you do not cover your skin.
- In mountainous areas there may be crevasses to fall into— use a stick to make sure the snow is solid.

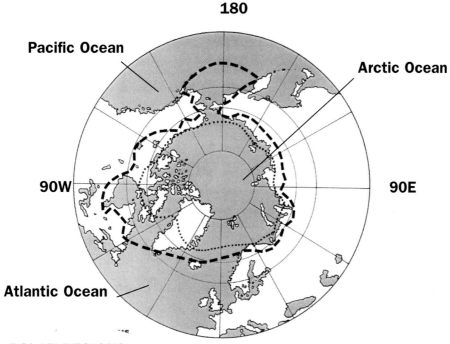

POLAR REGIONS
- - - - - SOUTHERN LIMIT OF LOW ARTIC TUNDRA
·········· SOUTHERN LIMIT OF HIGH TUNDRA AND POLAR BARRENS

northern Canada, freezing temperatures occur for six to seven months. In these conditions all moisture in the ground is frozen to a depth of several feet (a few meters).

Ice climates, in contrast, never get warm. The temperatures often never rise above 14°F (−10°C), and there is cloud cover for most of the year. There are three vast areas of ice on the Earth, which comprise the ice cap regions: Greenland, the Antarctic, and the Arctic.

The climates here are harsh in the extreme: vast rugged mountains, steep terrain, snow and ice fields, and glaciers. In addition to the incessant cold, the other great threat to survival is the wind. In the Antarctic, winds of up to 110 miles per hour (177 km/h) have been recorded. The combination of low temperatures and the wind creates a condition known as **windchill**. For example, a 20 miles per hour (32 km/h) wind will bring a temperature of 5°F (−14°C) down to −30°F (−34°C). This can pose great danger to the survivor: exposed flesh can freeze in seconds.

Both climates have seasonal extremes of darkness and daylight. Generally speaking, the nights of snow climate areas are long, even continuous, in winter. This can be a problem if you are a survivor for several reasons: no heat is received directly from the sun, and so the temperatures are very cold. The lack of light also restricts the amount of activity you can undertake outside your shelter, though the light from the moon, stars, and auroras (streamers of light playing across the clouds) reflecting off the white snowy ground do help. In addition, continued confinement in a cramped shelter can mean you start to get bored and depressed. In such a situation you must remember that the periods of complete darkness do not last long.

The polar regions are tough places to survive. But it can be done, and the Royal Marines know exactly how. Our first lesson from them will be how to build a shelter to protect ourselves from the biting cold and wind.

Blizzards are a combination of winds over 32 miles per hour (51 km/h) with enough snow to lower visibility to less than 500 feet (150 m).

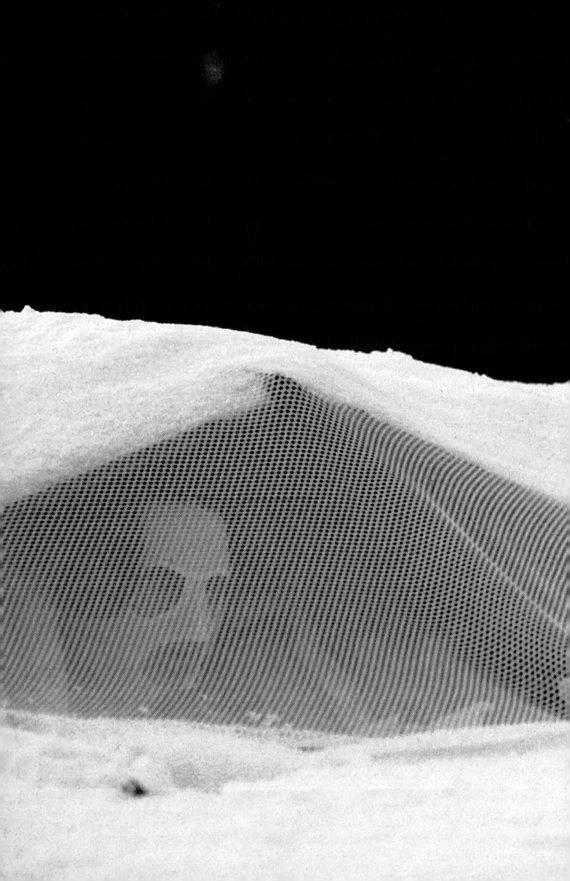

SHELTER

In arctic conditions, your first priority is to find a shelter from the freezing polar winds. If you can't find a shelter, then you are going to have to build one.

If you are in a polar region, it is very important that you get out of the wind and into some sort of shelter very quickly. The Royal Marines are experts in creating shelters using anything from branches and leaves to blocks of ice. One of the first things they teach you is to match the type of shelter you build to the terrain, natural resources available, weather, and snow conditions. Do not try to battle with nature; work in harmony with it. For example, if there are trees, you can build shelters using logs and tree trunks. If you are in the Arctic, away from trees, you will want to build a snow cave or snow trench. But whatever type of shelter you choose, remember to avoid the **leeward** side of cliffs where snow can drift and bury you, and areas where avalanches or rock falls are likely.

A Royal Marine in a place of deep snow will often make a snow shelter. To do this, you need a saw knife, snow knife, shovel, or machete to cut snow blocks. The snow from which you cut the blocks should be firm enough to support your weight. Try to find a place where drifts are deep enough to let you cut blocks from a vertical face. (It is less strenuous.) It is well worth spending time

This Marine's observation shelter features a mesh window, which will keep it well ventilated and lessen the chance of suffocation.

Marines construct a woodland shelter. Commando recruits spend about three months in the arctic snows of Norway.

finding proper snow of an even, firm structure, with no hollow or softer layers. The blocks should be around 18 by 20 inches (45 x 50 cm), and four to eight inches (10–20 cm) thick. Once cut, they can be built into a shelter.

When building shelters in snow and ice areas, the Royal Marines emphasize the following rules: Never lay a tool down in the snow; you will lose it. Never hurry; if you do, accidents and mistakes will happen. When building a shelter, drink as much water as possible because dehydration is a killer. Use as little energy as possible when building. Try to be as close as possible to the source of fuel for your fire. Take off clothes to keep cool during the physical activity of building. If you do not, your clothing will become soaked with sweat, and you will risk freezing. Always take time to plan where a shelter will be. For summer sheltering, remember that insects do not like wind, smoke, and plants such as yew. Always protect yourself from the cold and wet on the floor of your shelter with spruce boughs or some other form of **insulation.**

Regardless of the type of shelter you build in snow and ice areas, there are a number of Marine principles you must follow in order to make your stay in them as comfortable as possible. Don't have too many entrances to your shelter or you will lose heat. If you have to go outside, remember to gather fuel, insulating material, and snow or ice for melting. Do not waste your time. Try not to go outside to go to the bathroom. Instead, try to dig connecting snow caves, and use one as a bathroom. If that's not possible, use tin cans for urinals, and snow blocks for solid wastes. Always put thick insulation under yourself, even if you have a sleeping bag. Outer clothing makes good mattress material, while the shirt and inner pants can be rolled up and used as pillows. Keep sleeping bags dry, clean, and fluffed up. To dry a sleeping bag, turn it inside out, then beat out the frost and warm it in front of a fire. Be careful not to burn it. Brush all snow off clothes before entering a shelter. Snow on clothing will melt inside a warm shelter, and will then turn to ice when the clothing is taken outside. Remember: it is easier to keep clothing from getting wet than to dry it out later. If you are cold during the night, exercise by fluttering your feet up and down or by beating the inside of your sleeping bag with your hands.

We will now look at specific types of shelter that the Royal Marines use on survival exercises in snow and ice regions. With all of them, remember to watch out for snow gathering on the roof of your shelter—it may cause the roof to collapse when it gets too heavy.

Molded dome shelter

This is very quick and easy to construct. However, you do need some sort of large cloth or poncho with which to build it. Pile up bark or boughs (not too large), and cover these with a sheet of material (Fig 1). Then cover the material with snow. (Remember to leave a gap for an entrance.) When the snow has hardened, remove the cloth, bark, and twigs (Fig 2). Make an entrance block from a number of small sticks wrapped inside a piece of cloth, and then tied together (Fig 3). Remember to insulate the floor of the shelter with green boughs.

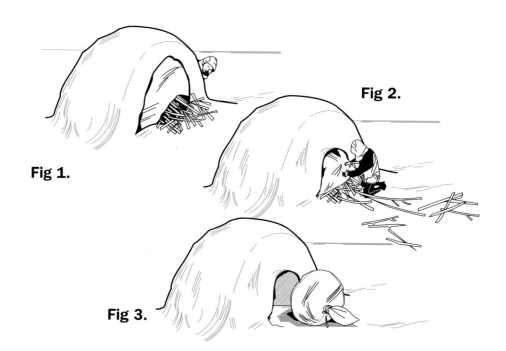

Fig 1.

Fig 2.

Fig 3.

Snow cave

A snow cave can be used in areas where you can find deep snow. Choose where you put the entrance carefully so that wind and more snow will not blow into it. Burrow a small tunnel into the side of the snow drift for three feet (90 cm). Then begin to dig out from this tunnel to the right and left at right angles to the tunnel entrance. You must ensure that the cave is high enough to sit up inside it. It should have an arched roof. This makes it stronger, and ensures that drops of water will run down the sides, and not drip on you. Try to make the area where you sleep higher than the tunnel entrance. Hot air rises, so this will be the warmest part of the shelter. The roof has to be at least one and a quarter inches (3 cm) thick, and the entrance should be blocked up with a backpack, poncho, or snow block to retain warmth. Remember to put an insulating material on the ground. The cave should have at least two ventilation holes: one in the roof and one in the door. Be especially careful to keep the cave ventilated if you are cooking or heating inside it.

Trench shelter

This is used by the Marines as a quick shelter that can give them some protection until they can build a better shelter. Find a large drift of snow and cut blocks. Make a trench just wider than a sleeping bag, and long enough for you to fit inside it. Build a wall of blocks around the trench and a roof with large slabs. (Hollow them slightly on the inside to form an arch.) Do not forget a ventilation hole. The trench shelter should not be used for too long. If you are going to be in the area for a long time, build an igloo.

A snow cave. Snowfall in arctic regions can be over one foot (30 cm) an hour, so you must make sure you do not get buried.

Igloo

Used by Inuits for centuries, and taught to the Royal Marines, the igloo is an excellent shelter in the polar regions. Draw a circle, 7 to 10 feet (2–3 m) on the snow. This works as a plan of your igloo. Cut 12 snow blocks. Now begin to build the igloo. The first row slopes inward, with the top edge of the blocks pointing down toward the center of the circle you have drawn (Fig 1). Now build up more blocks on the same principle until you are left with just a round hole at the top (Fig 2). This will take a disk of snow called a key block. When fitting the key block, the hole should be longer than it is wide to let you pass the key block up through the hole and then jiggle it into position (Fig 3). Then let it settle to close the hole. Build an entrance tunnel to complete the igloo (Fig 4).

Fig 1.

Fig 2.

Fig 3.

Fig 4.

Inside the igloo you should have a tunnel entrance to trap cold air, a cooking level, and a sleeping level. Put powdery snow on the dome and into open seams; it will harden and be an insulator. Do not forget to make some ventilation holes, and put insulating material on the

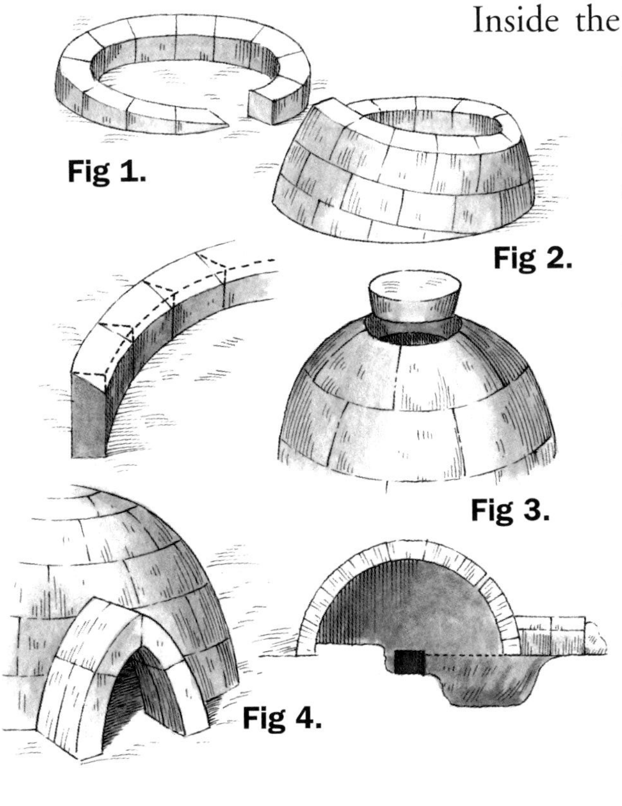

A step-by-step guide to constructing an igloo.

sleeping level. The cooking level must be reasonably close to the sleeping bench so anyone cooking does not have to rise from the bench. Be aware of high winds. If they are blowing, they can cause drifting snow to erode the wall of the igloo. A snow wall should be built to act as a windbreak. Inside the igloo, all sleeping bags should be placed side by side on the sleeping bench with their head end pointed toward the entrance. The igloo can be equipped with the following items:

- Stove: situate it near the entrance. Drive pegs into the wall above the stove, and hang pots from them.
- Drying rack: force sticks into the wall above the heat source. From these sticks you can dry clothing (always scrape snow off clothes before drying—never melt snow on garments), and thaw frozen foods.
- Door: use a snow block for the door. Keep it open during the day, and close it at night.
- Miniature igloo: build a smaller igloo at the side of the big one if you find the igloo is running out of space. Connect these two igloos with a small passage.

Inside the igloo you must not prepare food by frying, baking, or broiling. Heat canned goods in water.

Lean-to shelter

This shelter is easy to make, and can be both a summer or winter shelter. It will keep out insects, shield you from rain and snow, and keep you warm. Simply tie branches together in a grid pattern, and then lean this structure between two trees. Tie the top of the grid to the tree trunks. When you have built your framework, cover it with boughs, starting from the bottom and working your way up. Do not forget to insulate the floor. When you have constructed your shelter, add a door. You can even build another lean-to to face the first one you built if you have the time. Be imaginative.

With any shelter, you should always cover your floor with spruce or pine boughs to make a comfortable, dry sleeping area. Stones can be heated by the fire, and then placed inside the shelter to provide

MARINE TIPS FOR SHELTERING

The troops of the Royal Marines' Mountain and Arctic Warfare Cadre know better than anyone the importance of finding shelter in freezing climates. These are some of their tips:

- Do not sleep on bare ground. Use insulating materials such as spruce or pine boughs, dry grass, dried moss, or leaves.
- Do not cut wood that is too big for your shelter; it uses valuable energy.
- Do not scatter your equipment on the ground. Keep it in one place to stop you losing it.
- Have a fire going while you are building a shelter. It can be used as a heat source, a morale booster, and can provide boiling water for a hot drink.

The "A" shape of this shelter is stronger than a flat roof. The two halves push against one another under tension and hold it in place.

even more heat. (Put flat heated stones directly under the sleeping area, and cover them with more boughs to stop you from getting burned.) Try to keep your camp neat and tidy, and compact; you do not want to have to venture far from your shelter.

Always be sure that you have plenty of fuel supplies for your fire. Decide early on what type of fire you want. For example, if you build a log fire, you will have lots of warmth and light. However, it will burn quickly, and therefore requires lots of fuel. In a snowy area, you could use up a lot of physical and mental energy by having to gather fresh fire wood. Prepare your fire so that burns for a long time. The most important thing is that you do not let your fire go out, but keep it burning steadily.

Insects can be a problem in snow and ice areas, especially in summer. You may not even consider them when you are selecting a shelter site, but you should: they can make your life very hard. As a general rule, Royal Marines stay away from deep woods and pools of still water. This is where many insects live and are in their greatest numbers. Build your shelter where there is plenty of sunlight and a breeze—there will not be as many insects. If you are really being pestered by them (and insects can make the survivor's life unbearable), make a fire or a number of fires and be sure there is always some smoke around you. You may not like it very much, but the insects will like it a lot less. Use small fires with green or rotten damp wood to guarantee plenty of insect-repelling smoke.

By following the Royal Marine guidance on making shelters, you should be able to survive the worst weathers the arctic climate can throw at you. But to do this you also need fire.

MAKING FIRE

Every Royal Marine can make a fire with or without matches. These skills mean they can find warmth even in the middle of the polar snow and ice.

As a Royal Marine, you must learn how to make fire from the natural materials around you. Do not rely on matches—these can either be lost or become wet and useless. This chapter explains how the Royal Marines start and maintain fires in arctic conditions.

Fire is extremely important to the survivor. It can keep you warm and cheerful, dry your clothes, boil water, and be used for signaling and for cooking food. It is therefore vital that you know how to build and start a fire and keep it going. The three ingredients of a successful fire are air, heat, and fuel. The key to making a fire is to make sure all these ingredients are present. Be patient, and practice until you get it right. The materials for a fire fall into three categories: **tinder**, **kindling**, and fuel.

Tinder is any type of material that burns easily. It is usually thin, bone-dry fibers. Tinder includes shredded bark from some trees and bushes, crushed fibers from dead plants, fine, dry wood shavings, straw and grasses, sawdust, bird-nest linings, charred cloth, cotton balls or lint, steel wool, dry powdered sap from pine trees, paper, and

Human beings in Africa over 1,400,000 years ago used fire. But it wasn't until 7000 B.C. that humans could actually make fire.

All Royal Marines carry Meta-Tabs® in their arctic kit. These are small cubes of fuel, which are easily lit and can be used to start fires.

foam rubber. Get into the habit of always having tinder with you. Remember to carry it in a waterproof container. Kindling needs a higher temperature to burn and is added to the tinder. It is used to bring the burning temperature of the fire up to the point where bigger pieces of fuel can be added to the fire. Kindling includes dead, small, dry twigs; coniferous seed cones; pine straw; and wood that has been doused with flammable materials. Fuel doesn't have to be dry, but moist wood will produce a lot of smoke. The best fuel sources are dry, dead wood and the insides of fallen trees and large branches. Green wood can be split and mixed with dry wood to be used as fuel. If there are no trees, twist dry grass into bunches or use dried animal manure.

If you can, build a fire reflector. This is a wall made out of logs or rocks that directs, or reflects, the heat where you want it. Do not build a fire up against a rock. Instead, put it so you can sit between the rock and the fire. The rock will absorb warmth and keep your back warm.

One of the most important skills taught to Royal Marines is how to start a fire without matches. There are a number of easy ways to do this. When trying to start a fire, remember to do so out of the wind or with your back to the wind.

Flint and steel

Flint is a material that produces sparks when struck with metal. To start a fire using this, hold the flint and steel above the tinder. Strike the flint with the edge of the steel in a downward direction. The sparks must be fanned on the tinder and then further blown or fanned to produce a flame.

Burning glass

Focus the rays of the sun onto the tinder using a magnifying glass, a camera lens, the lens of a flashlight that magnifies, or even a piece of bottle glass.

Flashlight reflector

Place tinder in the center of the reflector where the bulb is usually located. Push it up from the back of the hole until the hottest light is concentrated on the end and smoke results.

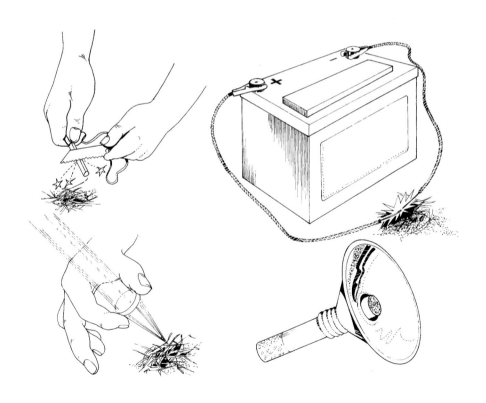

Ways to make fire without matches include a flint, a magnifying lens, a battery, and a flashlight.

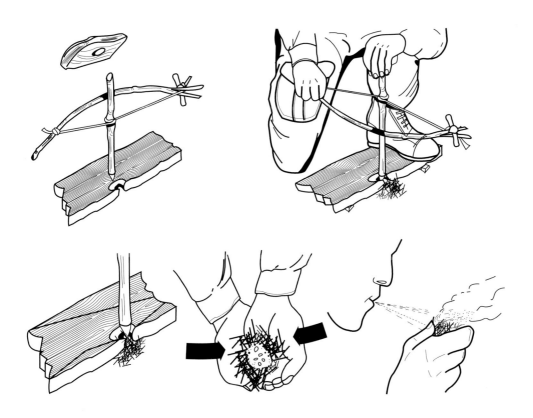

The bow-and-drill method relies on friction to work. Friction is the force that resists the movement of one object against another.

Bow and drill

This is an ancient method of making fire. Find a straight stick made from a hard wood around 12 to 18 inches (30–45 cm) long and three-quarters of an inch (2 cm) across. Make one end round and sharpen the other into a blunt point. The round end fits into a hole in another piece of wood—called a socket—which can be held comfortably in one hand. Put grease or soap in the hole to prevent heat from building up. The bow should be made from a

A shelter protects from frostbite and hypothermia. This soldier dries out his gloves over a fire, which will help to keep him warm.

ROYAL MARINES FIRECRAFT TIPS

- Save your matches for starting properly prepared fires, and use them sparingly.
- Always try to carry dry tinder in a waterproof container.
- In the Arctic, a platform will be needed to prevent a fire from melting down through deep snow and putting it out.
- You will also need a platform if you start a fire in an area of peat or humus to stop it from spreading—a smoldering peat fire can burn for years.
- In woods, clear away debris to prevent fire from spreading.

branch around three feet (90 cm) long and one inch (2.5 cm) in diameter. Tie a piece of string to both ends so the whole thing looks like the bow from a bow and arrow.

Then you have to make what is known as a fireboard. This is where the fire will actually start. The fireboard is a piece of flat softwood around 12 inches (30 cm) long and three-quarters of an inch (2 cm) thick and three to six inches (7.5–15 cm) wide. Carve a small hollow in it, then make a V-shaped cut in from the edge of the board. This cut should go into the center of the hollow. While kneeling on one knee, place the other foot on the fireboard and place tinder just beneath the V-cut. Rest the board on two sticks to create the space. (This lets air into the tinder, which it needs in order to burn.)

Twist the string of the bow once around the stick and place the stick with the sharp end into the hollow. Then press the socket down on the stick and fireboard. Spin the stick with long, even strokes of the bow until you see smoke, then spin faster to make thick smoke. By this stage, the friction has made a hot powder out of the wood. The bow and stick can then be removed and tinder placed next to the glowing wood powder. Roll tinder around the burning ember and blow on it to burn the tinder. The burning tinder is then placed in a waiting fire containing more tinder and small kindling.

Now we know how the Royal Marines make fire. But it is also important to choose a good spot for your fire. The Marines give this advice: Choose a sheltered site. Do not light a fire at the base of a stump or tree. Clear away all debris on the ground in a circle at least six feet (1.8 m) across until you reveal bare earth. If the ground is wet or covered with snow, build the fire on a platform constructed from green logs covered with a layer of earth or stones. In strong winds, dig a trench and light a fire in it. In windy conditions, encircle your fire with rocks. In the Arctic, a platform will be needed to prevent fire from melting down through deep snow and putting itself out.

Being able to make fire is essential to polar survival. Yet the Marine must be careful. Fire is always dangerous. Do not place wet rocks or stones near fires—they can explode when heated. Test all rocks by banging them together. Do not use any that crack, sound hollow, or flake, and avoid slates and soft rocks. If rocks contain moisture, the moisture will expand faster than the rocks when heated, and the rocks may explode. If they do explode, they can fire off dangerous pieces of bulletlike stones.

One of the main reasons for making fire is to cook. The Royal Marines are experts in finding and catching food, and this is the lesson of the next chapter.

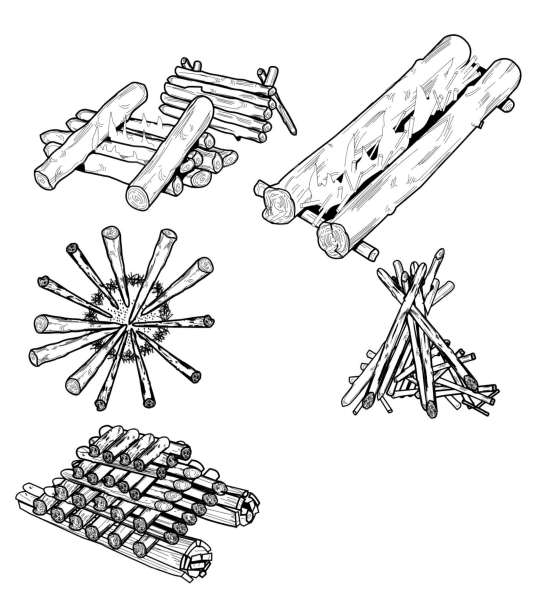

Fire lays control the amount of oxygen getting to a fire. For instance, if the lay is very open, the fire will burn quickly.

FINDING FOOD

Stranded in arctic conditions, the Royal Marines need to find food fast if they are to survive for any length of time. Luckily their training has taught them how to do this like experts.

No matter how fit they are, Royal Marines need a constant supply of food and water to keep themselves going in polar regions. Fortunately, there is plenty of water in these places in the form of streams, lakes, ponds, snow, and ice. But remember: do not eat unmelted snow or ice. This lowers the body's temperature and can lead to various types of illnesses. A Royal Marine's method for melting snow or ice is a water machine. Place snow on any material that water can flow through (like a cotton T-shirt). Gather up the edges so you have a bag of snow. Hang this from a branch over a container near a fire. The heat will melt the snow and the water will drip from the bag into the container. Water may be easy to find, but the Marine will have to hunt harder for food. In snow and ice areas there are many available types of food, both plant and animal. However, a Marine needs to know where these food sources are, and when they are available.

Plants are a good source of food. The following arctic and northern plants should be part of a Marine's survival diet, especially lichens, which have sustained many survivors in cold climates.

A Marine skins a rabbit for food. Rabbits are prolific animals, producing 4 to 12 young about seven times a year.

Red spruce

Appearance: this tree is up to 70 feet (21 m) in height and has yellow-green needles around its hairy twigs. *Edible parts*: young shoots can be eaten raw or cooked. Eat the inner bark after boiling.

Black spruce

Appearance: this is smaller than the red spruce with shorter needles. *Edible parts*: young shoots can be eaten raw or cooked. Eat the inner bark after boiling.

Ferns are actually one of the world's oldest life forms. Fossil evidence shows that ferns were growing on Earth 408 million years ago.

Labrador tea

Appearance: an evergreen shrub with an average height of one to three feet (30–90 cm). It has narrow leaves with rolled edges, whitish or gray underneath, and five-petaled white flowers. *Edible parts*: the leaves make a refreshing tea.

Arctic willow

Appearance: round leaves, shiny on top, and yellow catkins. *Edible parts*: the spring shoots, leaves, inner bark, and peeled roots are all edible.

Ferns

Appearance: green, leafy plants. *Edible part*: eat only the young fiddleheads up to six inches (15 cm) long. Steaming is the best way to cook these. (Hang them over a steaming container of boiling water for about 20–30 minutes.)

Iceland moss

Appearance: leathery, with gray-green or brownish mats up to four inches (10 cm) high, made up of many small branches. *Edible parts*: soak all parts for several hours, and then boil thoroughly. Found exclusively in the Arctic in open areas.

Bearberry

Appearance: woody, with evergreen leathery leaves, pink or white flowers, and clusters of red berries. *Edible parts*: the entire plant is edible when cooked.

Salmonberries can form a succulent food. Only eat berries that are ripe and soft, as hard berries are difficult to digest.

Salmonberry

Appearance: looks like a small wild raspberry. Has thornless, three-part leaves, purplish-red flowers, and juicy red or yellow flowers. *Edible parts*: the berries can be eaten raw.

Reindeer moss

Appearance: this is a lichen that grows two to four inches (5–10 cm) high in large clumps with hollow, round, grayish stems, and branches that resemble reindeer antlers. *Edible parts*: soak all parts for several hours and then boil thoroughly.

Rock tripes

Appearance: lichens that form roundish, blisterlike grayish or brownish growths attached to rocks. *Edible parts*: soak all parts for several hours, then boil thoroughly.

These plants will help a Royal Marine to keep hunger and starvation at bay. Yet a more important source of food is animals, though they can be difficult to catch. There are many animals that can provide a food source in snow and ice areas. Marines must remember that some of the larger ones can be dangerous. They will usually avoid these unless they have their guns with them. There are several types of animal to be found in the polar regions. Ones that the Marine should avoid are wolves, bears, and walruses. These are very dangerous creatures, particularly if they are injured. There are other large animals like caribou, reindeer, and musk oxen. These provide plenty of food if caught, but without a gun a Marine probably won't attempt to kill them because of their dangerous antlers. Sheep can be found in many snow regions. In the winter they go down to the valleys and lower areas, and they are an excellent source of food. The same is true of arctic hares, marmots, lemmings,

All parts of the rock tripe are edible.

ducks, geese, grouse, and seals. Always cook meat thoroughly, and do not eat the livers of seals or polar bears—they contain dangerous chemicals.

Catching animal food is a difficult skill. Of course, it is made more easy using a gun. Yet Marines must know what to do if they have lost their guns or are out of ammunition. Snares are probably the easiest trap. A snare is a wire or string loop. It is placed so that an animal is forced to put its head through it, such as outside the entrance to a rabbit warren. The snare will then tighten, thus killing the animal (though sometimes not immediately). Bear in mind that the material you make the snare out of has to be strong enough to catch its intended prey. Another type is the deadfall trap. The principle of these traps is simple: when the bait is taken, a weight falls on the prey and kills it.

The animal touches or trips a line,

A walrus can weigh up to 2,770 pounds (1,260 kg).

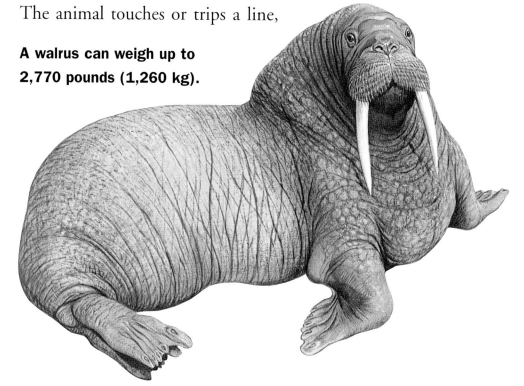

Caribou can stand up to 56 inches (1.4 m) at the shoulder. They make an excellent food source.

stick, or pole. This is connected to a heavy weight, which then falls on the animal. Spear traps can also be very effective. They consist of a springy piece of wood, bent under tension and held in place by a wire. This piece of wood has a spear firmly lashed to it, which hits the animal when it is released.

Fish are an excellent food in watery areas. When lakes are frozen, fish usually gather in the deepest water. Cut through the ice at this point and bait a fish hook. Make a pennant from cloth or paper and attach it to a light stick. Tie this firmly at right angles to another stick that is longer than the width of the hole in the ice. Fasten the fishing line to the other end of the flagpole, and rest the pennant on the side of the hole. When a fish takes the bait, the flagpole will be jerked upright.

In any survival situation, you must take food when and where you find it. Do not wait. For example, you may stumble across a

A Marine sniper goes hunting. His rifle is the Accuracy International L96A1, which has its wooden parts camouflaged white.

The arctic fox is a burrow dweller. It is grayish-brown during the summer months but turns pure white in the winter.

herd of caribou. In this situation you may think that you have time on your hands—you don't! Caribou are migratory animals and they are probably just passing through the area. When you wake up tomorrow they may all be gone, and you will have lost a valuable food source. Therefore you must try to kill as many as possible. But now you have a problem: how will you stop the meat from rotting?

If it is winter, you can freeze the meat. In fact, your main problem will be getting the skin off as quickly as possible and cutting the meat up into sections. You should prepare and store food from animals by skinning the animal first. Cut the meat into small sections. After doing this, you need to store it. Build a platform off the ground. Place the meat on it and cover it with boughs to keep birds away. Do not build this platform in your camp. In the summer it may attract bears, and the last thing you want is a bear sniffing around your camp looking for food.

Unless you are going to eat the meat immediately, you will want to preserve it. Cooling helps keep meat fresh. Cut the meat into sections and hang them in a cool place out of the sun. The air will start to dry the outside of the meat. Start a number of smoky fires to smoke the meat. Do not let the fires heat the meat; just smoke it. (Do not use **conifer** wood—it ruins the flavor.) Smoked meat, if kept dry, can be stored in this condition for a long time. Dry smoking keeps the meat even longer. Cut the meat up into long, thin strips, and hang it on a drying rack. Dry the meat out in sunlight or with a fire. At the same time, have a smoky hardwood fire going. When the meat seems dry, move it nearer the fire for a few minutes to raise the temperature of the meat. When the strips are hot to the touch, move them back from the fire and continue to dry them until they become brittle. You can chew on them or cook them in water to rehydrate them.

Also, you can make a saltwater solution and soak the meat in it before drying. To make this, fill a container with seawater and bring it to a boil. Add more seawater as the water in the container evaporates. Then fill the container to the top again and let it cool. Do not use unboiled seawater; it does not contain enough salt to be sterile. The meat will obviously taste salty, but it will keep for even longer periods.

Though the polar regions may look like there is no food there, Royal Marines are trained to find plenty to eat. They are also trained to find their way through the confusing and often featureless landscape, the subject of our next chapter.

The Arctic has about six months of twilight in the winter. Also, each year there are 24-hour periods when the sun does not rise or set.

TRAVELING AND NAVIGATION

Never get lost in polar climates—you might not make it out alive. The Royal Marines know exactly how to keep going in the right direction.

It is difficult to travel in the polar regions. Deep snow makes walking exhausting. Blizzards can reduce visibility to only a few feet and blot out the sun. Shifting ice can mean that it is hard to walk in one direction for long. Royal Marine training faces these problems, and each Marine knows the rules of survival travel.

Because of the tough polar environment, movement should be made only if you are in danger. The decision to travel when in a survival predicament should be based on the likelihood that you can reach safety before rescuers are able to find you—so do not move if you are near a large object like a crash-landed plane.

Other factors include the weather and whether you are ill or injured. You should not venture out in a blizzard or, if a blizzard is coming, you must be aware that travel will involve plenty of physical exertion. This means an increased amount of food and water. You will also need to be able to build temporary shelters en route. If you are moving by foot, you will be able to take with you only what you can carry. You will burn off a lot of energy and sweat more water than normal. So make sure that you can find food or water on your journey.

A ski patrol sets off. Skiing is an ancient practice, and in northern Europe skis have been found that date back 4,000 to 5,000 years.

The freezing waters of the arctic are lethal for the survivor. If you fall in, you will have only about three minutes before losing consciousness.

If you decide to leave camp, place a marker to show the rescue crews where you have gone. The **snow-block shadow signal** is the best signal in snow conditions. Simply build up snow in a large tall arrow flat on the ground. It should be as large as possible in an open area and should point exactly in the direction you intend to travel. Also carry a reflector in a handy place in case an aircraft appears, or carry fire-starting material in your pocket to start a signal fire.

Choose your route carefully at the beginning of each day. You do not want to get cold and wet by going through swamps and bogs. Try to follow running water if possible. That's because many communities live on a river or stream. If you follow water, you will be able to replace the fluids you lose through exertion. There will be fish in the river or stream, and animals will be attracted to it to drink, giving you the opportunity of catching them. In addition, there will probably be many edible plants growing alongside it.

When following a waterway, don't build a raft and float on it. Many northern rivers are fast, cold, and dangerous, and can smash a raft into splinters. You do not know the river, and even if one appears calm, remember that there could be rocks under the water that could tear your raft to pieces in seconds. Also, when crossing

Arctic ground is in a state called permafrost, meaning it is permanently frozen. Only the top inch or two (2.5–5 cm) of the soil will ever defrost.

thin ice, lie flat and crawl so as to distribute your weight and reduce the risk of falling through it.

You must bear the following points in mind when navigating in snow and ice areas: In winter, long nights, blowing snow, and fog limit visibility. Snowfalls can obliterate tracks and landmarks, making it much easier to lose your way. There is limited daylight in the winter. Compass readings are unreliable because of the poles' magnetic fields. Large-scale maps could be nonexistent for the area you are in. You may encounter a multitude of lakes, ponds, and creeks that are not on your map. This can be confusing and can lengthen travel times.

Marines using the latest navigational tools. The soldier on the right wears a face mask to protect his skin from frostbite.

Global Positioning System (GPS) use satellites orbiting the Earth to pinpoint locations. They are accurate to within 32 feet (10 m).

The arctic air is very clear, which makes it difficult to estimate distances, as in deserts. You are in danger of underestimating distances since objects appear closer than they actually are. Make camp early to leave adequate time to build a shelter. Use snowshoes if the snow is deep. These can be made out of willow, and they look like a tennis racket that can be fitted to your feet.

You will need to be able to work out where you are as well as your intended route. There are a variety of signs that the Royal Marines use to navigate. In the northern hemisphere, true north can be gauged from the constellation of Ursa Major (Great Bear), which points to the North Star (Polaris), standing over the North Pole. In the southern hemisphere, the Southern Cross indicates the direction of south. In the daytime, if you have the correct local time, the shadow cast by a straight object stuck straight up in the ground at midday will indicate north and south. Clouds over snowless ground or water will appear black, while clouds over snow or sea ice will be white. Pack ice and drifted snow will create a mottled effect in the clouds. Seabirds generally fly out to sea in the morning and return to land at night. Moss will be thickest on the north side of rocks or trees. Alder bark is lighter on the south side. Lichens are more numerous on the south side.

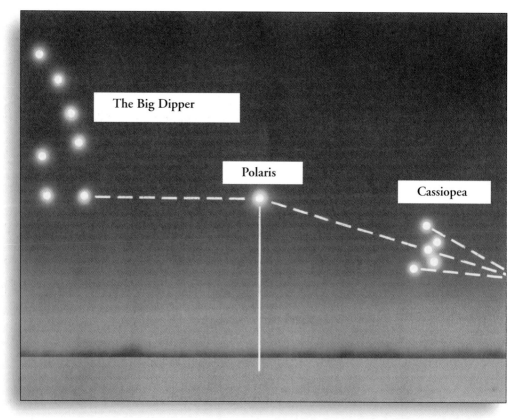

Finding the North Star (Polaris). The two stars at the end of the Big Dipper which point to Polaris are called Merak and Dubhe.

MARINE NAVIGATIONAL TIPS

- When traveling on sea ice, do not use icebergs or distant sea landmarks to get your bearings. The positions of these objects can change.
- Avoid icebergs, which have most of their mass below the water. They can turn over without warning, especially with your weight on them.
- Do not sail close to ice cliffs. Thousands of tons of ice may fall into the sea without warning.
- Migrating wildfowl fly to land in the thaw, and most seabirds fly out to sea during the day and return at night, thereby indicating land.
- Clouds appear black underneath when over open water, timber, or snow-free ground, and white over the sea ice and snow fields. New ice produces grayish reflections.

During arctic warfare, the Royal Marines would use the best in sophisticated navigational equipment to track the enemy. But they must know how to survive without it. Using their navigational knowledge, the Royal Marines can guide themselves through snowy arctic wastes without getting lost.

So far, this book has shown how the Royal Marines can build shelters, make fire, and acquire food. But we must not overlook the fact that one of the most important things the Marines must do when going to the polar regions is choose their clothes wisely.

CLOTHING

Your clothing is vital to help you survive the arctic elements. The Royal Marines will teach you exactly what you need to wear to increase your chances of survival.

Royal Marines have specialized uniforms to help them survive in polar weather. While we do not have these uniforms, there are several vital principles the Marines teach for what clothes you should wear. You should protect the whole body from the cold and wind, especially the head and feet. By keeping active, you will keep the blood circulating in your body. However, try not to sweat. If you do, loosen or remove some clothing. Try to keep clothing clean; dirt and grease clog the air spaces in your clothing and reduce insulation. Try to wear goggles: they will stop you from getting snow blindness.

Traveling on foot through snow and ice can be exhausting. Skiing is best on snow with a hard crust, but snowshoes are better for deep, loose snow. You can fashion tree branches to make a pair of snowshoes. When you walk with the shoes on, the binding should hinge at the toe so you can drag the tail end. Also, remember to protect your fingers. Keep your hands covered. Do not place them on metal when extremely cold because you will get a cold burn. If your hands get cold, place them inside your clothing under your armpits, next to your stomach, or between your thighs.

This soldier is wearing arctic clothing, including special mittens that let him fire his gun, while still keeping his hands warm.

The **layer principle** offers the maximum protection from your clothing. The principle is very simple: still air is the best form of insulation, and the best way of creating it is to trap it between layers of clothing. The more layers you wear, the greater the insulating effect. Temperature control is very easy; all you do is add or take away layers according to how much protection you need.

Skies are generally best for walking through snow with a hard crust, but snowshoes are preferable if the snow is loose and deep.

When skiing cross-country, soldiers uses skis that are narrower than those used to go down mountains.

This SBS Marine wears a one-piece waterproof immersion suit under his clothing to protect him from freezing arctic waters if he were to fall in.

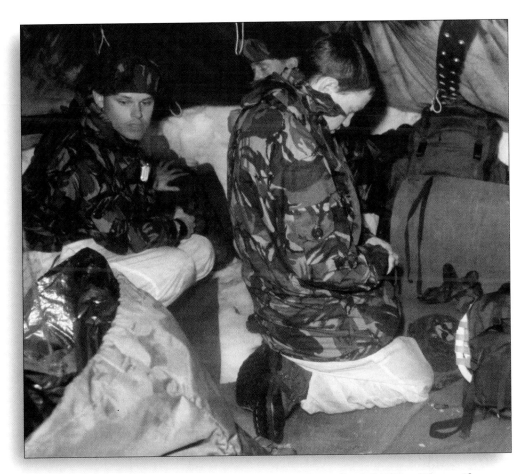

The pattern on these soldiers' uniforms is called DPM—Disruptive Pattern Material—the standard camouflage of the British Army.

Remember, getting too hot can be as much of a problem as being cold. If you sweat when it's cold, the body chills when you stop sweating, and your sweat-soaked clothing will draw away body heat into the air. It is important that you prevent this with proper clothing. You should wear several layers. Next to the skin, wear thermal underwear. Over this, wear a woolen or wool mixture shirt. On top of this, wear a woolen or good fiber-pile sweater or jacket (fiber-pile tends to be better because it is warmer and more

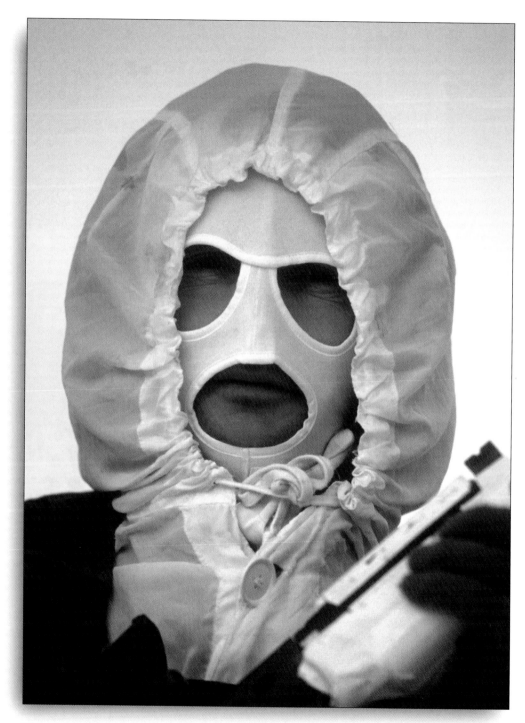

This M&AW Cadre soldier is wearing a protective snowsuit that is waterproof, windproof, and also offers full-face camouflage.

windproof), then have a fiber-pile down or Holofil® (synthetic material) jacket. The final layer must be windproof and waterproof.

For any outdoor activity, it is best to equip yourself with a pair of waterproof boots. Royal Marines never wear running shoes in polar regions; they will not protect you from the cold and wet. The best kind of footwear is walking boots with a flexible sole and

A soldier takes aim with his SA80 assault rifle. He is using his skis to rest his weapon on to improve his accuracy.

Of course, one of the best ways to stay warm and dry is to build a shelter. A willow frame shelter is effective in arctic conditions.

a deep tread. Britain's Royal Marines are very concerned with the care of their boots because they have to "yomp," or march, long distances on foot. When their boots become wet they dry them by stuffing them with newspapers, which absorb the moisture, and leaving them in a warm place. They prevent laces from snapping in cold weather by rubbing wax over them

Your boots should be big enough to let you wear two or three pairs of socks underneath. Socks that are too tight will restrict the blood circulation and the layer of warm air that is between them—this can lead to frozen feet. Always carry a spare pair of socks. Whenever your feet get wet, change your socks as quickly as possible to prevent sores.

It is important to look after your boots, and it is always wise to carry a spare pair of laces around with you. Protect the boot with wax or polish, and always check your boots for any damage before you use them. Remember, if you look after your boots, they will look after you. Socks are another important item of footwear. Choose

Water freezes almost instantly in the polar regions—look at the frozen tears on this soldier's eyelashes for proof!

ones that are very warm. Marines wear two pairs on their feet for comfort and to prevent blisters.

Windproof pants are recommended for outdoor use, but they should also be light and quick drying. Some have around five pockets with zippers, making them excellent for carrying items securely. Over these you can wear waterproof pants. These should have a side zipper or be wide enough to let them be put on if you are wearing a pair of boots. Be careful they are not too tight. If they are, your legs will quickly start to sweat.

Your jacket forms your outer layer. It must be windproof and waterproof. A jacket with a covered zipper is best. This will prevent the wind and rain from entering, and will be a backup if the zipper fails. The jacket should have a deep hood big enough to cover a hat. It should also cover the lower part of the face for further protection. The sleeves should cover the hands, and the jacket should have wrist fasteners. It should also be big enough to go over several layers of clothing. The number of jacket pockets is a personal choice, but you should choose a jacket that has at least two on the outside with waterproof flaps and one inside that can hold a map. The jacket should be knee-length and also have drawcords at the waist and hem.

Color is a matter of choice. Royal Marines often wear white snowsuits to make them harder to be seen by the enemy. However, for survival you should wear bright colors to draw attention to yourself if rescuers are out looking for you. A jacket is one of your most important items of clothing, if not the most important. Do not compromise when it comes to buying one. Paying a little bit more for a good jacket will get you an item that may save your life.

TRICKS FOR STAYING WARM

- Put elastic bands around your wrists and ankles to make sure that no heat is lost from flapping clothing.
- Newspaper is an excellent insulator. In an emergency, putting sheets of it inside your clothing will give you some protection from extreme winds.
- At the end of the day, try to find a safe period when you can take off your jacket and fleece and "fluff" it up by shaking it. If clothes become very flat from wearing them, then they will not be as warm as they should be.

Protecting your hands and head requires gloves and a hat. There are many woolen and ski gloves for sale, but mittens are warmer. However, they can be very clumsy if you want to use your fingers. Therefore, wear a thin pair of gloves under your mittens. It is estimated that between 40 and 50 percent of heat loss from the body can occur through the head, so it is important to wear a good hat. Any sort of woolen hat or **balaclava** will help prevent heat loss, though of course they are not waterproof.

As any Royal Marine will tell you, good clothing is vital for surviving in polar regions. Learn from them, and get the best you can when going into arctic conditions. Yet for all your clothing, the polar weather can still harm you. We will now let the Royal Marines teach us how to survive the dangers of the arctic environment when disaster strikes.

DANGERS AND FIRST AID

If you get ill in the arctic, your chances of survival are not good. However, if you act fast, and use Royal Marine training, the chances of coming through are much, much better.

The polar regions are full of dangers that the Royal Marine must face with courage and skill. The main danger is the intense cold. You must get out of the cold and the wind immediately and build a shelter. Otherwise you could find yourself falling victim to a wide range of illnesses, including **dehydration**, **hypothermia**, **frostbite**, sunburn, and **trench foot**.

The first indication that you are dehydrated is the color of your urine: it will appear very dark yellow. Other symptoms are no appetite, feeling slow and heavy, drowsiness, and a temperature higher than normal. You must drink plenty of liquids—water, tea, soup—in cold weather to avoid dehydration.

Hypothermia happens when the center of the body cools below its normal temperature of 97 to 100°F (36–38°C). It is life-threatening. The symptoms are (in order): mild shivering; uncontrollable shivering (you will have difficulty controlling your fingers and hands); violent shivering (difficulty speaking); shivering slows down and stops; strange behavior; inability to make decisions; unconsciousness; and then death. Keep watch for any signs of

In summer, when ice thaws, the sudden release of water can make mountain rivers rise by up to 16 feet (5 m) in only a few hours.

shivering. Be particularly alert for when the shivering slows down or stops. This is a critical warning. The treatment for hypothermia is heat. Stop what you are doing and get out of the cold. Build a fire, get dry, drink warm fluids, eat chocolate. If you come across a person who is hypothermic, get him or her out of the wind and into shelter. Remove wet clothing and replace with dry items. Place warm rocks or water bottles filled with warm water near the patient's throat, armpits, and groin. Build a fire to provide heat.

Trench foot is an injury many Royal Marines had to fight in the Falklands War. It is caused by the feet being constantly cold and wet. In the early stages, feet and toes appear pale and feel numb, cold, and stiff. Walking is difficult, and the feet swell and become painful. You must be alert to prevent trench foot; it can lead to amputation. To prevent trench foot, make sure you clean and dry your socks and boots regularly, and dry your feet as quickly as possible if they get wet. If wearing wet boots and socks, exercise your feet continually by wriggling your toes and bending your ankles. Get out of the wet footwear as quickly as possible. When treating trench foot, handle the feet very gently. Do not rub or massage them. Clean carefully with soap and water, dry, and then raise them up. Do not walk if you have trench foot.

Frostbite is broken down into three types: frostnip, superficial frostbite, and deep frostbite. It can be very serious, leading to the loss of toes, fingers, arms, legs, and life. It occurs when part of your body—usually your fingers, toes, ears, or nose—start to freeze in the cold. With frostnip, the skin turns white but there is no pain. Superficial frostbite is more serious. It strikes fingers, hands, toes,

Wet boots increase the chances of frostbitten feet. Marines wear waterproof gaiters over the entire boot, which stops the water entering.

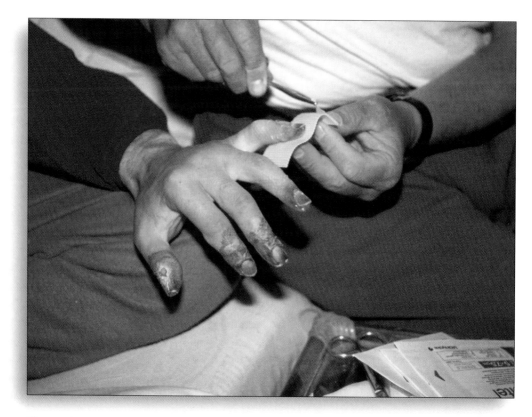

Frostbite is an excruciatingly painful condition which can result in the loss of fingers and toes if not treated quickly.

feet, and face, but sometimes knees and upper legs. The skin appears white, waxy, and solid. The area will be numb, and may have a blue or purple outline. Deep frostbite is a complete freezing of a part of the body. The affected area will be white and hard, and completely numb.

To treat frostnip: cover the affected area and keep it dry and warm. To treat other frostbite: never thaw a frozen body part if there is a chance it will become frozen again. When you are in a safe location, you can thaw the affected parts. Gently soak in water that is kept at a temperature of 100 to 110°F (36–41°C)—it feels warm to the touch. The flesh should turn to pink or red; at this point, the victim will experience extreme pain. Large blisters will form in a day; do not burst them. They will break on their own in two to three weeks. With deep frostbite, a hard black shell will form over the area. Leave it; it is protecting damaged tissue and will come off in three to six weeks. The area should heal totally within six months to a year. Remember: do not thaw slowly in cold water; do not thaw by holding close to a fire; do not rub the area, especially with snow.

A serious danger to Royal Marines is falling through ice. Part of their training involves them jumping through an ice hole into freezing water and then clawing their way out using ski poles. If you fall into water you must act quickly; otherwise you could be dead within minutes. The icy water will literally knock the breath out of you, and you will lose control of your muscles and shiver violently. As soon as you fall into the water, move as quickly as you can for

Heat is lost more quickly into cold ground than cold air. That's why this hypothermia victim has been placed on a layer of branches.

land. Once on land, roll in the snow to absorb water, get to shelter, and into dry clothes. Speed is vital.

Though you might not think it, another danger in the polar regions is sunburn. This is because the rays of the sun reflect upward from snow and ice. Vulnerable areas are lips, eyelids, and nose. Apply sunblock to these areas (including the inside of your nose). Your eyes are also vulnerable. Wear sunglasses. If you do go snow blind, your eyes will be red and sore; they will water, and you will have a headache. Treatment includes blindfolding yourself and waiting until the soreness goes away. If you don't have sunglasses, improvise a pair from cardboard or tree bark: cut small slits and look through these.

The ultimate arctic training—a tough Marine soldier goes plunging through an ice hole with full pack and has to get out by himself.

A fully grown polar bear can weigh anything up to 1,600 pounds (720 kg).

Rubbing charcoal (from logs burned in your fire, but wait until they are cool) onto the skin around the eyes will also help to reduce glare.

Animals are another danger. Bears are present in the northern forests and wastes. Steer clear of them; they are powerful and dangerous and can kill. Polar bears are found in the high Arctic and they are powerful and tireless creatures that can pursue you for miles. Other animals to be avoided are walruses and elephant seals.

There are certain plants that the Royal Marines know not to eat. Do not eat water hemlock, baneberry fruit, arctic buttercups, lupin, larkspur, locoweed, false hellebore, or death camas. They are all very poisonous. Use a good plant book to identify these before you set out on your journey.

Another danger, which many do not know about, is called carbon monoxide poisoning. Carbon monoxide is a poisonous chemical that has no color or smell. It will be given off by any gas or stove. This is particularly dangerous in extremely cold climates because shelters are likely to be small and well sealed against the elements. Without plenty of fresh air coming in, the carbon monoxide can build up to dangerous levels.

The symptoms of carbon monoxide poisoning are difficult to detect, especially when they are happening to you. They include slight headache, dizziness, drowsiness, nausea, and perhaps vomiting.

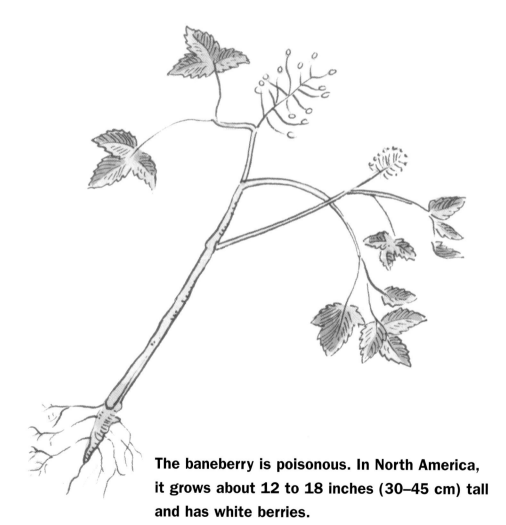

The baneberry is poisonous. In North America, it grows about 12 to 18 inches (30–45 cm) tall and has white berries.

HYGIENE IN POLAR REGIONS

For many reasons, it's important that you stay as clean as possible when you are in a survival situation. A clean body holds its heat better and stays healthier, and clean clothes offer better protection against the cold and wind. The Marines have the following recommendations:

- Change your socks and wash your feet every day. This helps prevent trench foot from setting in.
- Clean your teeth daily to stop dental problems developing.
- Change your underwear at least twice a week. If it is not possible to wash it, crumple it and shake it, then air it for at least two hours.

The victim may also suddenly fall unconscious. To treat, remove the patient to fresh air or a well-ventilated area and get him or her to breathe deeply. If unconscious, apply artificial respiration in a well-ventilated area. (Learn this from a good first-aid course or book.) Give oxygen if available. When recovered, the patient should be allowed to rest and be given warm drinks. The patient should not undertake heavy work until fully recovered.

To prevent carbon monoxide poisoning, make sure that there are at least two ventilation holes in your shelter to let fresh air enter. Do not let fires burn up too high. Turn off all stoves and lamps before going to sleep.

Most of the injuries and dangers can be easily prevented. The Marines treat the arctic wastes with caution, and so should anyone who is attempting to survive in such extreme cold.

The Royal Marines have made polar survival their specialty. They are tough and resourceful soldiers. We have talked about many survival techniques in this book, yet the Royal Marines also teach us that courage, a good sense of humor, and optimism are vital to surviving in the freezing arctic conditions. If you think the environment can beat you, it probably will. If you believe you can survive, then your chances of coming through are good.

Marines are careful when holding pieces of metal—like this gun. In extreme climates, it can stick to exposed skin and tear off flesh.

Skiing often results in broken bones. Bones are strongest when you are young. After age 50, human bones become increasingly brittle.

GLOSSARY

Amphibious Involving forces landed from the sea.

Antarctica The polar ice cap that forms the southern cap of the Earth.

Arctic The polar ice cap that forms the northern cap of the Earth.

Atlantic Wall The German fortifications along the coast of France in World War II, parts of which were attacked by the Royal Marines during the Dieppe raid.

Balaclava A tight woolen garment covering the head and neck except for parts of the face.

Blizzards Polar storms that feature very high winds, heavy snow, and "whiteout" conditions where visibility is almost zero.

Cold War A period of sustained hostility between on one side the United States and the U.S.S.R on the other. The situation lasted from the end of World War II until the late 1980s without either side ever resorting to military conflict.

Conifer A tree bearing cones and needle-like leaves.

D-Day The Allied invasion of German-occupied France on June 6, 1944, which eventually led to the defeat of Nazi Germany.

Dehydration An illness that occurs when people lose more of their body's water than they take in through drink.

Dieppe A disastrous mission against the German coastal defenses of occupied France, in which the Royal Marines played a vital role.

Frostbite The name for a condition where parts of the body freeze in extreme cold, usually the fingers, toes, nose, and ears.

Hypothermia A serious medical problem in which the victim's body temperature falls below a safe level.

Insulation Anything that keeps in warmth and keeps out the cold.

Kindling Any material used to start a fire, usually small dry twigs, bark, or dry grass.

Layer principle The warmest way to wear clothes by putting on many different layers; each layer traps in the heat.

Leeward Being in or facing the direction toward which the wind is blowing.

Mountain and Arctic Warfare Cadre An elite unit within the Royal Marines, specially trained to fight in freezing climates.

Snow-block shadow signals Signals made by building up snow into tall shapes that can be seen by rescue aircraft flying over.

Special Boat Service An elite unit specializing in amphibious operations.

Tinder A flammable substance that can be used as kindling to start a fire. Dried leaves is an example of tinder.

Trench foot A serious condition in which the feet become swollen and rotten from spending too long being wet and in boots.

Tundra A harsh, desolate polar landscape with permanently frozen soil.

Windchill The effect the wind has of making temperatures much colder than if the air was calm.

EQUIPMENT REQUIREMENTS

Headwear
Balaclava helmet
Woolen/thermal hat
Face protector

Clothing
Waterproof/windproof outer jacket
Thermal underjacket/fleece
Waterproof pants
Thermal underclothes
Many pairs of socks
Snow goggles

Footwear
Walking boots
Gaiters
Spare laces
Crampons
Skis
Snowshoes

Load-carrying Equipment
Backpack
Small carry sack
(Both must be waterproof.)

Survival Equipment
Medical pack
Mess pack and knife/fork/spoon
Water bottle and mug
Survival knife
Lockable/retractable knife
Tent
Climbing and walking ropes
Sleeping bag
Plastic sheeting (to build
   shelters/make solar stills)
Sleeping mat
Survival bag
Telescopic walking stick or ski stick
Shovel/spade (foldable)
Compass
Watch
Chronograph
Flares
Signaling mirror (heliograph)
Binoculars
Map case
Wash pack
Matches
Flint and steel firelighter
Snare wire
Water purification tablets
Fishing gear
Whistle
Candle (some candles are made to
   be edible)

CHRONOLOGY

October 28, 1664	Britain's first Marine unit formed, called the Duke of York and Albany's Maritime Regiment of Foot.
1755	The Marines are given the name HM Marine forces.
1802	The Marines finally receive the official title Royal Marines.
1804	The Royal Marine Artillery (RMA) are formed.
1855	The Royal Marines Light Infantry (RMLI) are formed.
1856–1900	Royal Marines fight for many years in China and Japan.
1914–1918	World War I. The Royal Marines fight on the Western Front.
1923	The RMA and RMLI are brought together to form the Corps of Royal Marines.
1939–1945	World War II. The Royal Marines fight throughout the war in Europe and the Far East.
1942	The Royal Marine Commandos are formed.
August 1943	RM Commandos take part in the raid on German coastal defenses at Dieppe in occupied France.
June 6, 1944	The Royal Marines storm ashore with the Allied forces during the D-Day landings at Normandy.
1956	RM Commandos take part in an Anglo-French operation against Egyptian forces around the Suez Canal.
1960–1967	Royal Marines operate in Aden in the Middle East against various revolutionary armies.
1962–1966	Royal Marines fight in the jungles of the Federation of Malaysia.
1969	Royal Marines begin foot patrols on the dangerous streets of Northern Ireland. This job would continue for several decades.
1982	The Falklands War. Royal Marines play a vital role in

	freeing the island, and suffer 27 men killed and 67 wounded.
1991–1992	Royal Marines deployed to the Middle East as part of the Allied force during the Gulf War.
1994–95	Royal Marine units are sent to Bosnia-Herzegovina on peacekeeping operation.
1995–Present Day	Royal Marines continue to serve with the NATO Implementation Force.
2000–2001	Marines help British forces in peacekeeping operations in Kosovo and Sierra Leone.

RECRUITMENT INFORMATION

Entrance to the Royal Marines is very tough because there are only 7,000 Royal Marines in total, and standards are high. The academic grades needed are not too difficult—five GCSEs (the standard examination for 16-year-olds in the U.K.)—but the actual training is incredibly hard. The recruit training center is at Lympstone in Devon, southwest England. The training program itself last 36 weeks and includes exercises such as 30-mile speed marches in seven and a half hours carrying 30 pounds (14 kg) of kit and a rifle. Obviously you need to be very fit. Seventy-five percent of people who join the basic training do not make it to the end.

To join the Royal Marines, you must be a U.K. citizen. Any Royal Navy recruitment office (there is usually one in every major town and city in the U.K.) will be able to handle your application.

For more information visit the following websites:
http://www.specialoperations.com/foreign/United_Kingdom/
   Royal_Marines/Mountain_Leader.htm
http://www.royal-navy.mod.uk
http://www.royalmarinesmuseum.co.uk
http://www.reserveforces.london.org.uk
http://www.British_Royal_Marines.com

FURTHER READING

Cobb, Norma and Charles Sasser. *Arctic Homestead: The True Story of One Family's Story of Courage and Survival in the Alaska Wilds*. New York: St. Martin's Press, 2000.

Lane, Andrew. *The Royal Marines Commandos in the Falklands*. Devon, England: Halsgrove, 2000.

McManners, Hugh. *The Complete Wilderness Training Book*. London: DK Publishing, 1999.

McNab, Chris. *First Aid Survival Manual*. Edison, N.J.: Chartwell Books, 2001.

Molvar, Erik and Elayne Sears. *Alaska on Foot: Wilderness Techniques for the Far North*. Woodstock, Ver.: Countryman Press, 1996.

Swaney, Deanna. *Lonely Planet. The Arctic—A Travel Survival Kit*. London: Lonely Planet, 1999.

Thompson, Julian. *The Royal Marines*. London: Pan, 2001.

Wiseman, John. *The SAS Survival Handbook*. New York: HarperCollins, 1996.

ABOUT THE AUTHOR

Dr. Chris McNab has written and edited numerous books on military history and elite forces survival. His publications to date include *German Paratroopers of World War II*, *The Illustrated History of the Vietnam War*, *First Aid Survival Manual*, and *Special Forces Endurance Techniques*, as well as many articles and features in other works. Forthcoming publications include books on the SAS, while Chris's wider research interests lie in literature and ancient history. Chris lives in South Wales, U.K.

INDEX

References in italics refer to illustrations

Accuracy International L96A1 rifle *54*
amphibious assaults 12
　Special Boat Service (SBS) 15–17
animals 19
　as food *47*, 51–56
　dangerous 85
　see also insects
antitank rockets
　MILAN antitank rockets *14*
arctic fox *55*
arctic willow 49
armored vehicles
　BV202 armored vehicle *16*
arms *see* weapons
Atlantic Wall 10–12

backpacks 92
balaclavas 77
battles see fighting
bearberry 49
birds 19
black spruce 48
blizzards *23*, 59
boats 12
　Landing Craft Assault (LCA) vehicle *11*
boots 73–75
bow and drill
　to light fires 41–44
BV202 armored vehicle *16*

camouflage *71*
carbon monoxide poisoning 85–87
caribou *53*, 55
chronology 93–94
cleanliness
　clothes 67, 87
　teeth 87
climate 19–23
clothing 26–27, *42*, 67–77, 92
　for insulation 27
　green berets 17
Cold War 14
compasses 21, 62
conflict *see* fighting
cookers 32

D-Day landings 10
dangers
　animals 85
　carbon monoxide poisoning 85–87
　dehydration 26, 79
　frostbite 80–83
　hypothermia 79–80, 83
　ice, falling through 83–84
　plants 85
　sunburn 84–85
　trench foot 80
dehydration 26, 79
Disruptive Pattern Material *71*
drinking water *see* water

drying racks 32
Dutch Wars 9

eating *see* food
equipment requirements 92

Falkland Islands 12–14
ferns 49
fighting
　Cold War 14
　Dutch Wars 9
　Falkland Islands 12–14
　Malaysia and Indonesia 12
　Suez Canal, Egypt 12
　World War I 9–10
　World War II 10–12
finding your way *see* navigation
fires 37–45
　fuel for 26, 27, 35
　to smoke meat 56
first aid
　carbon monoxide poisoning 86–87
　dehydration 79
　frostbite 80–83
　hypothermia 79–80, 83
　ice, falling through 83–84
　sunburn 84–85
　trench foot 80
fish
　as food 53, 61
flashlight reflectors 40
flints 39
food, finding 46–57
footwear 92
　boots 73–75
　snowshoes 63, 67, *68*
frostbite 80–83
fuel for fires 26, 27, 35, 37–39

glass
　to light fires 40
Global Positioning Systems (GPS) *63*
glossary 90–91
gloves *42*, 67, 77
goggles 67
green berets 17
guns *see* weapons

headwear 77, 92
heat loss 77
helicopters
　in Egypt 12
　Westland Sea King *20*
history of the Royal Marines 9–17
　chronology 93–94
hygiene *see* cleanliness
hypothermia 79–80, *83*

ice climates 22–23
ice, falling through 83–84
Iceland moss 49
igloos 31–32

illness *see* first aid
immersion suits *70*
Indonesia 12
injuries *see* first aid
insects 35
　mosquitoes 21

jackets 71–73, 76

L4A4 machine gun *13*
labrador tea 49
Landing Craft Assault (LCA) vehicle *11*
lean-to shelters 32–33
list of equipment 92

machine guns
　L4A4 machine gun *13*
Malaysia 12
marching 74
medicine *see* first aid
Meta-Tabs 38
MILAN antitank rockets *14*
Molded Dome Shelters 28
mosquitoes 21
Mountain and Arctic Warfare Cadre (M&AW) *6*, 15, 72
　tips for shelters 33

navigation
　compasses 21, 62
　Royal Marine tips 65
　stars 63–64
　streams 60–61
Norway
　training in 14, 17

observation shelters *25*

pants, windproof 76
perspiration 26–27, 67, 71
plants 19, 20
　as food 47–51
　dangerous 85, *86*
　to build shelters 33
polar bears 85
polar regions 19–23
preserving meat 56

rabbits, as food *47*
recruitment information 94
red spruce 48
reindeer moss 50
rifles
　Accuracy International L96A1 rifle *54*
　SA80 assault rifle *73*
rivers
　for navigation 60–61
rock tripes 51

SA80 assault rifle *73*
salmonberry 50
seacraft *see* boats
shelters 24–35, *42*
　willow frame shelters *74*
shirts 71
sickness *see* first aid

signaling
　snow-block shadow signals 60
skiing *58*, 67, *69*, *89*
sleeping bags 27
snares 52–53
snow caves 29, *30*
snow climates 20–22
snow shelters 25–26
snow-block shadow signals 60
snowshoes 63, 67, *68*
snowsuits 72, 76
socks 74–76
Special Boat Service (SBS) *15*, 15–17
stars, for navigation 63–64
stoves, in igloos 32
streams
　for navigation 60–61
Suez Canal, Egypt 12
sunburn 84–85
sunglasses 84–85
survival equipment list 92
sweaters 71
sweating *see* perspiration

tanks
　in Egypt 12
thermal underwear 71
Thompson submachine gun *10*
toilets 27
traps
　for catching food 52–53
traveling 59–65
trench foot 80
trench shelters 29

underwear 71

vegetation *see* plants

walrus *52*
warmth
　from clothing 77
　see also fires
wars *see* fighting
washing *see* cleanliness
water
　dehydration 26, 79
　for navigation 60–61
　to drink 47
weapons
　Accuracy International L96A1 rifle *54*
　L4A4 machine gun *13*
　MILAN antitank rockets *14*
　SA80 assault rifle *73*
　Thompson submachine gun *10*
weather 19–23
Westland Sea King helicopter *20*
willow frame shelters *74*
windchill 22
woodland shelters *26*
World War I 9–10
World War II 10–12